PROGRAM NOTE

Based on folk melodies and other songs collected by the composer from various regions of China, *Seven Tunes Heard in China* was written for cellist Yo-Yo Ma. It was commissioned by the Pacific Symphony for Dr. George Cheng in honor of his wife Arlene Cheng, to whom the work is dedicated. The movements and their sources are as follows:

I. Seasons (Qinghai)

Spring is coming,
Narcissi are blooming,
The maiden is out from her boudoir seeking,
My love boy, lend me a hand, please.

II. Guessing Song (Yunnan)

Baby, I am testing you:
What is the long, long thing in the sky?
What is the long, long thing under the sea?
What is the long, long thing sold on the
  street?
What is the long, long thing in front of you,
  young girl?

III. The Little Cabbage (Hebei)

The little cabbage is turning yellow on the
  ground,
She lost her parents when she was two or
  three.
Mom, my Mom!

IV. The Drunken Fisherman

Classical, based on a tune originally written for the *qin*, an ancient seven-string Chinese zither.

V. Diu Diu Dong (Taiwan)

The train is coming,
It is going through the tunnel!

VI. Pastoral Ballade (Mongolia)

White clouds are floating in the blue, blue sky;
Under the clouds, the grass is covered by
  the snow-white sheep.

The sheep are like pieces of white silver,
Spreading over the green, green grass.
How lovely!

VII. Tibetan Dance

Based on a well-known Tibetan folk dance.

first performance of Seven Tunes Heard in China:
Yo-Yo Ma, cello, October 9, 1995
Cheng Hall, Irvine Barclay Theatre, Los Angeles

recording available on compact disc:
Yo-Yo Ma – Solo
(*Sony Classical* SK 64110)

duration: ca. 20 minutes

PERFORMANCE NOTES

1. All grace notes occur on the beat.

2. A solid line between pitches indicates *glissando*.

   glissando occurs at very end of first note value

   glissando occurs immediately

BRIGHT SHENG

SEVEN TUNES HEARD IN CHINA

for solo cello

edited by Yo-Yo Ma

ED 4087

first printing: April 2001

ISBN 0-7935-9830-3

G. SCHIRMER, *Inc.*

DISTRIBUTED BY

HAL•LEONARD®
CORPORATION

7777 W. BLUEMOUND RD. P.O. BOX 13819 MILWAUKEE, WI 53213

SEVEN TUNES HEARD IN CHINA
for solo cello

I. Seasons

Bright Sheng
edited by Yo-Yo Ma

II. Guessing Song

III. Little Cabbage

♩ = 58–60

IV. The Drunken Fisherman

Elegantly and in tempo ♩ = 40

* ▽ Use a guitar pluck or a plastic card (e.g. a credit card) to pluck the notes under the sign.

4

♩ = 84 (poco più mosso)

* ⌒ Nail pizz., near bridge.

V. Diu Diu Dong

* 〰〰〰 Wide vibrato.

VI. Pastoral Ballade

to Yo-Yo

VII. Tibetan Dance

♩ = 132–138

* L.H. tapping the cello body.

* Approximate pitches.